MAD⊙LIBS®

MAD LIBS FROM OUTER SPACE

By Roger Price and Leonard Stern

PSS!
PRICE STERN SLOAN

ISBN 0-8431-2443-1

2001 Printing

MAD☺LIBS®
INSTRUCTIONS

**MAD LIBS® is a game for people who don't like games!
It can be played by one, two, three, four, or forty.**

• RIDICULOUSLY SIMPLE DIRECTIONS

In this tablet you will find stories containing blank spaces where words are left out. One player, the READER, selects one of these stories. The READER does not tell anyone what the story is about. Instead, he/she asks the other players, the WRITERS, to give him/her words. These words are used to fill in the blank spaces in the story.

• TO PLAY

The READER asks each WRITER in turn to call out a word—an adjective or a noun or whatever the space calls for—and uses them to fill in the blank spaces in the story. The result is a MAD LIBS® game.

When the READER then reads the completed MAD LIBS® game to the other players, they will discover that they have written a story that is fantastic, screamingly funny, shocking, silly, crazy, or just plain dumb—depending upon which words each WRITER called out.

• EXAMPLE (*Before* and *After*)

" _____ !" he said _____
           EXCLAMATION   ADVERB

as he jumped into his convertible _____ and
                                              NOUN

drove off with his _____ wife.
                              ADJECTIVE

" *Ouch!* !" he said *Stupidly*
           EXCLAMATION   ADVERB

as he jumped into his convertible *cat* and
                                              NOUN

drove off with his *brave* wife.
                              ADJECTIVE

In case you have forgotten what adjectives, adverbs, nouns, and verbs are, here is a quick review:

An ADJECTIVE describes something or somebody. *Lumpy, soft, ugly, messy,* and *short* are adjectives.

An ADVERB tells how something is done. It modifies a verb and usually ends in "ly." *Modestly, stupidly, greedily,* and *carefully* are adverbs.

A NOUN is the name of a person, place or thing. *Sidewalk, umbrella, bridle, bathtub,* and *nose* are nouns.

A VERB is an action word. *Run, pitch, jump,* and *swim* are verbs. Put the verbs in past tense if the directions say PAST TENSE. *Ran, pitched, jumped,* and *swam* are verbs in the past tense.

When we ask for a PLACE, we mean any sort of place: a country or city *(Spain, Cleveland)* or a room *(bathroom, kitchen.)*

An EXCLAMATION or SILLY WORD is any sort of funny sound, gasp, grunt, or outcry, like *Wow!, Ouch!, Whomp!, Ick!,* and *Gadzooks!*

When we ask for specific words, like a NUMBER, a COLOR, an ANIMAL, or a PART OF THE BODY, we mean a word that is one of those things, like *seven, blue, horse,* or *head.*

When we ask for a PLURAL, it means more than one. For example, *cat* pluralized is *cats.*

MAD LIBS® is fun to play with friends, but you can also play it by yourself! To begin with, DO NOT look at the story on the page below. Fill in the blanks on this page with the words called for. Then, using the words you have selected, fill in the blank spaces in the story.

Now you've created your own hilarious MAD LIBS® game!

COPERNICUS

ADJECTIVE_____

NOUN _____

PLURAL NOUN _____

NATIONALITY _____

SOMETHING ROUND _____

NUMBER _____

LAST NAME OF PERSON _____

ADJECTIVE_____

PERSON IN ROOM _____

TYPE OF FOOD_____

NOUN _____

OCCUPATION _____

ADJECTIVE_____

ADVERB_____

VERB ENDING IN "ING" _____

VERB _____

MAD LIBS®
COPERNICUS

Four hundred years ago, people knew little about our _____
ADJECTIVE

universe. They thought that the earth was the center of the entire

_____ and that the sun and all of the _____
NOUN   PLURAL NOUN

revolved around it. But then a/an _____
NATIONALITY

named Copernicus discovered the truth. The earth revolves around

the _____ _____ times a year.
SOMETHING ROUND   NUMBER

Copernicus, whose last name was _____, was born in
LAST NAME OF PERSON

Warsaw, and he used one of the first _____ telescopes,
ADJECTIVE

which was invented by _____. This primitive
PERSON IN ROOM

telescope was little more than two pieces of _____ stuck
TYPE OF FOOD

on each end of a/an _____.
NOUN

In 1600, an Italian _____ named Galileo expanded
OCCUPATION

Copernicus' _____ theories. But during the Inquisition
ADJECTIVE

in Italy, he was _____ arrested. After _____
ADVERB   VERB ENDING IN "ING"

for six months in jail, Galileo was forced to _____.
VERB

From MAD LIBS® FROM OUTER SPACE • Copyright © 1989 by Price Stern Sloan,
a division of Penguin Putnam Books for Young Readers, New York.

MAD LIBS® is fun to play with friends, but you can also play it by yourself! To begin with, DO NOT look at the story on the page below. Fill in the blanks on this page with the words called for. Then, using the words you have selected, fill in the blank spaces in the story.

Now you've created your own hilarious MAD LIBS® game!

OUR SOLAR SYSTEM

ADJECTIVE _____

NOUN _____

ADJECTIVE _____

PLURAL NOUN _____

ADVERB _____

VERB ENDING IN "ING" _____

SILLY WORD (PLURAL) _____

ADJECTIVE _____

PLURAL NOUN _____

FIRST NAME _____

ADJECTIVE _____

NUMBER _____

ANOTHER FIRST NAME _____

ANOTHER FIRST NAME _____

ANOTHER FIRST NAME _____

ANOTHER FIRST NAME _____

ANOTHER FIRST NAME _____

ANOTHER FIRST NAME _____

PLURAL NOUN _____

MAD LIBS®
OUR SOLAR SYSTEM

When we look up into the sky on a/an _____ summer
ADJECTIVE

night, we see millions of tiny spots of light. Each one represents a/an

_____ which is the center of a/an _____
NOUN   ADJECTIVE

solar system with dozens of _____ revolving
PLURAL NOUN

_____ around a distant sun. Sometimes these suns expand and
ADVERB

begin _____ their neighbors. Soon they will become so
VERB ENDING IN "ING"

big, they will turn into _____. Eventually they subside
SILLY WORD (PLURAL)

and become _____ giants or perhaps black _____.
ADJECTIVE   PLURAL NOUN

Our own planet, which we call _____, circles around
FIRST NAME

our _____ sun _____ times every year. There are eight other
ADJECTIVE   NUMBER

planets in our solar system. They are named _____,
ANOTHER FIRST NAME

_____, _____, _____,
ANOTHER FIRST NAME   ANOTHER FIRST NAME   ANOTHER FIRST NAME

_____, _____, Jupiter, and Mars. Scientists
ANOTHER FIRST NAME   ANOTHER FIRST NAME

who study these planets are called _____.
PLURAL NOUN

From MAD LIBS® FROM OUTER SPACE • Copyright © 1989 by Price Stern Sloan,
a division of Penguin Putnam Books for Young Readers, New York.

MAD LIBS® is fun to play with friends, but you can also play it by yourself! To begin with, DO NOT look at the story on the page below. Fill in the blanks on this page with the words called for. Then, using the words you have selected, fill in the blank spaces in the story.

Now you've created your own hilarious MAD LIBS® game!

MOON WALK

VERB ENDING IN "ING" _____

NUMBER _____

PERSON IN ROOM _____

NOUN _____

ANOTHER PERSON IN ROOM _____

ADJECTIVE_____

PLURAL NOUN _____

ANOTHER PERSON IN ROOM _____

PROFESSION _____

ADJECTIVE_____

COLOR_____

PLURAL NOUN _____

TYPE OF DAIRY FOOD _____

MAD LIBS®
MOON WALK

The greatest true-life space story is the one about our astronauts

_____ to the moon for the first time.
VERB ENDING IN "ING"

There were _____ astronauts. We all remember their names:
NUMBER

_____, who was the expert in _____;
PERSON IN ROOM   NOUN

_____, a/an _____ test pilot with a
ANOTHER PERSON IN ROOM   ADJECTIVE

Ph.D. in _____; and _____, who
PLURAL NOUN   ANOTHER PERSON IN ROOM

was the ship's _____ and conducted a series
PROFESSION

of really _____ experiments with _____
ADJECTIVE   COLOR

mice and _____. It was a great day for America
PLURAL NOUN

when they landed and said, "Whatta ya know? It really is made out

of _____."
TYPE OF DAIRY FOOD

From MAD LIBS® FROM OUTER SPACE • Copyright © 1989 by Price Stern Sloan,
a division of Penguin Putnam Books for Young Readers, New York.

MAD LIBS® is fun to play with friends, but you can also play it by yourself! To begin with, DO NOT look at the story on the page below. Fill in the blanks on this page with the words called for. Then, using the words you have selected, fill in the blank spaces in the story.

Now you've created your own hilarious MAD LIBS® game!

CAPTAIN ZOOM I

NOUN _____

COLOR _____

COLOR _____

ADJECTIVE _____

TYPE OF FOOD _____

TYPE OF LIQUID _____

NUMBER _____

PLURAL NOUN _____

ADJECTIVE _____

ADVERB _____

COLOR _____

PLACE _____

ADJECTIVE _____

NUMBER _____

PERSON IN ROOM (MALE) _____

SILLY WORD _____

ADVERB _____

MAD LIBS®
CAPTAIN ZOOM I

The adventures of Captain Zoom, Space _____. Captain
                                        NOUN

Zoom is a superhero who wears a/an _____ cape and
                                        COLOR

a/an _____ suit of long underwear. He has his own
                 COLOR

_____ rocket ship, which takes him all over the universe.
ADJECTIVE

His ship is fueled by _____ mixed with _____
                      TYPE OF OOD   TYPE OF LIQUID

and can go _____ miles per hour.
               NUMBER

Captain Zoom loves to go to the assistance of poor _____
                                             PLURAL NOUN

who are in trouble. When he hears of such a/an _____
                                      ADJECTIVE

situation, he leaps _____ into his ship and zooms off into
                   ADVERB

the wild _____ yonder. He journeys throughout the galaxy,
          COLOR

sometimes going as far as _____. He has a/an _____
                         PLACE   ADJECTIVE

companion who goes with him on all of his adventures.

His companion is a _____-year-old boy whose name is
                        NUMBER

_____ but who is called "_____."
PERSON IN ROOM (MALE)   SILLY WORD

To read more about Captain Zoom, _____ go to the
                                       ADVERB

next Mad Lib.

From MAD LIBS® FROM OUTER SPACE • Copyright © 1989 by Price Stern Sloan,
a division of Penguin Putnam Books for Young Readers, New York.

MAD LIBS® is fun to play with friends, but you can also play it by yourself! To begin with, DO NOT look at the story on the page below. Fill in the blanks on this page with the words called for. Then, using the words you have selected, fill in the blank spaces in the story.

Now you've created your own hilarious MAD LIBS® game!

CAPTAIN ZOOM II

NATIONALITY _____

PLURAL NOUN _____

PLURAL NOUN _____

TYPE OF CONTAINER _____

ADJECTIVE_____

ADJECTIVE_____

PLACE _____

VERB ENDING IN "ING" _____

EXCLAMATION_____

NOUN _____

SOMETHING ALIVE _____

ADJECTIVE_____

VERB (PAST TENSE)_____

ADVERB_____

PLURAL NOUN _____

MAD LIBS®
CAPTAIN ZOOM II

One day Captain Zoom heard that a group of _____

NATIONALITY

_____ had been picked up by some little green

PLURAL NOUN

_____ who were in a flying saucer. He learned they

PLURAL NOUN

were locked in a/an _____ on the _____

TYPE OF CONTAINER   ADJECTIVE

planet Hang-On.

At once he called to his _____ companion, "Hey, Shorty,

ADJECTIVE

get the spacecraft warmed up. We are going to _____."

PLACE

And off they zoomed, _____ around the moon and

VERB ENDING IN "ING"

past Mars. In no time at all they landed on Hang-On. When Captain

Zoom stepped out of his ship, he said, " _____ !"

EXCLAMATION

because the first thing he saw was a purple _____ which

NOUN

was eating a long, thin _____. He whipped out his Super

SOMETHING ALIVE

_____ Ray Gun and blasted away until he had _____

ADJECTIVE   VERB (PAST TENSE)

everything in sight. "Now, Shorty," he said _____ , "let's

ADVERB

see if we can find some _____ to rescue."

PLURAL NOUN

MAD LIBS® is fun to play with friends, but you can also play it by yourself! To begin with, DO NOT look at the story on the page below. Fill in the blanks on this page with the words called for. Then, using the words you have selected, fill in the blank spaces in the story.

Now you've created your own hilarious MAD LIBS® game!

CAPTAIN ZOOM III

NOUN _____

ADJECTIVE _____

ADJECTIVE _____

TYPE OF GAS _____

TYPE OF LIQUID _____

NUMBER _____

COLOR _____

ANOTHER COLOR _____

NUMBER _____

NUMBER _____

NOUN _____

TYPE OF FOOD (PLURAL) _____

PLURAL NOUN _____

PART OF THE BODY (PLURAL) _____

TOWN _____

ADVERB _____

ADJECTIVE _____

MAD LIBS®
CAPTAIN ZOOM III

After zapping everything he could see around his spaceship with his

Alpha Particle Disintegrator _____, Captain Zoom began
                                    NOUN

to explore the _____ planet Hang-On. Hang-On had
                      ADJECTIVE

a/an _____ atmosphere containing lots of _____
          ADJECTIVE   TYPE OF GAS

and _____. The natives were about _____ feet tall and
      TYPE OF LIQUID   NUMBER

were _____ except for their hair, which was _____.
        COLOR   ANOTHER COLOR

They had _____ arms and _____ fingers on each _____.
            NUMBER   NUMBER   NOUN

They lived by growing _____ and fertilizing them
                          TYPE OF FOOD (PLURAL)

with _____. They welcomed Captain Zoom with
          PLURAL NOUN

open _____. They took him to their capital city,
        PART OF THE BODY (PLURAL)

called _____, and said they wanted to make him
            TOWN

their king. "I couldn't," he said _____,"because
                                        ADVERB

I am a/an _____ American."
              ADJECTIVE

From MAD LIBS® FROM OUTER SPACE • Copyright © 1989 by Price Stern Sloan,
a division of Penguin Putnam Books for Young Readers, New York.

MAD LIBS® is fun to play with friends, but you can also play it by yourself! To begin with, DO NOT look at the story on the page below. Fill in the blanks on this page with the words called for. Then, using the words you have selected, fill in the blank spaces in the story.

Now you've created your own hilarious MAD LIBS® game!

CAPTAIN ZOOM IV

NOUN _____

ADJECTIVE_____

NOUN _____

VERB _____

EXCLAMATION_____

ADVERB_____

PLURAL NOUN _____

EMOTION_____

TYPE OF BUILDING _____

VERB (PAST TENSE)_____

SOMETHING ON THE DINNER TABLE _____

ADJECTIVE_____

TYPE OF VEHICLE _____

NOUN _____

ADVERB_____

MAD LIBS®
CAPTAIN ZOOM IV

"Although I cannot be your _____ King," Captain Zoom told
                                    NOUN

the _____ natives of Hang-On, "I will be your
                  ADJECTIVE

_____ . And I will _____ you like a father."
        NOUN   VERB

At this, the natives cheered. " _____ !" they shouted
                                        EXCLAMATION

_____ . And they began pelting the good captain with
          ADVERB

overripe _____ , which was how they showed respect and
              PLURAL NOUN

_____ . Then they took him to their local _____
    EMOTION   TYPE OF BUILDING

and released all of the earth people they had _____
                                                      VERB (PAST TENSE)

with their flying _____ . So Captain Zoom
                        SOMETHING ON THE DINNER TABLE

put them all on his _____ space _____ ,
                          ADJECTIVE   TYPE OF VEHICLE

set it for " _____ "Warp, and went back to Earth. They
                    NOUN

all lived _____ ever after.
                ADVERB

MAD LIBS® is fun to play with friends, but you can also play it by yourself! To begin with, DO NOT look at the story on the page below. Fill in the blanks on this page with the words called for. Then, using the words you have selected, fill in the blank spaces in the story.

Now you've created your own hilarious MAD LIBS® game!

LETTER FROM A MARTIAN

NOUN _____

NOUN _____

ADJECTIVE _____

VERB _____

ADJECTIVE _____

NAME OF PERSON _____

ADJECTIVE _____

VERB _____

VERB ENDING IN "ING" _____

NOUN _____

PLURAL NOUN _____

NOUN _____

MAD LIBS®
LETTER FROM A MARTIAN

Dear Earthling:

I am a teenage _____ who lives in a two-story
                         NOUN

_____ on Mars. I will put this letter in a/an
         NOUN

_____ bottle and _____ it into space and
   ADJECTIVE   VERB

hope that it gets to Earth.

Of course, on Mars we call your _____ planet
                                         ADJECTIVE

_____. We know that it is inhabited by _____
NAME OF PERSON   ADJECTIVE

little pink men and women, but I would like to hear from you any-

way. Tell me, how do you people _____ your food?
                                      VERB

We do it by _____ rapidly.
              VERB ENDING IN "ING"

I hope you will be able to visit me someday. You could stay in our

_____ and eat _____ just like we do, and you
      NOUN   PLURAL NOUN

could play with my pet _____ .
                              NOUN

MAD LIBS® is fun to play with friends, but you can also play it by yourself! To begin with, DO NOT look at the story on the page below. Fill in the blanks on this page with the words called for. Then, using the words you have selected, fill in the blank spaces in the story.

Now you've created your own hilarious MAD LIBS® game!

THE SPACESHIP

VERB ENDING IN "ING" _____

PLURAL NOUN _____

NUMBER _____

NUMBER _____

ADJECTIVE _____

ADJECTIVE _____

NOUN _____

ARTICLE OF CLOTHING _____

NUMBER _____

TYPE OF METAL _____

ADJECTIVE _____

PLURAL NOUN _____

ADJECTIVE _____

TYPE OF GAS _____

ANOTHER TYPE OF GAS _____

ADVERB _____

VERB _____

MAD LIBS®
THE SPACESHIP

A spaceship is a vehicle used for _____ people

VERB ENDING IN "ING"

between Earth and the distant _____. A journey

PLURAL NOUN

usually takes _____ years and can cover _____ miles. The

NUMBER ... NUMBER

passengers have to enter a/an _____ capsule and will

ADJECTIVE

exist in a state of _____ animation. When the ship reaches

ADJECTIVE

its destination, they will hear a/an _____ and wake up and

NOUN

put on their _____. Then they have to land their

ARTICLE OF CLOTHING

_____-ton _____ vehicle in a/an _____

NUMBER ... TYPE OF METAL ... ADJECTIVE

atmosphere. They do this by firing the retro _____.

PLURAL NOUN

Then they test the atmosphere on this _____ planet to make

ADJECTIVE

sure it contains _____ and is not all _____.

TYPE OF GAS ... ANOTHER TYPE OF GAS

If it is okay, they can get out of the ship very _____ and

ADVERB

_____ all of the inhabitants.

VERB

MAD LIBS® is fun to play with friends, but you can also play it by yourself! To begin with, DO NOT look at the story on the page below. Fill in the blanks on this page with the words called for. Then, using the words you have selected, fill in the blank spaces in the story.

Now you've created your own hilarious MAD LIBS® game!

NEWSPAPER STORY

TOWN_____

VERB ENDING IN "ING" _____

NOUN _____

TOWN_____

NAME OF PERSON (MALE)_____

TYPE OF VEHICLE _____

PLURAL NOUN _____

COLOR_____

NOUN _____

SOMETHING ALIVE (PLURAL) _____

PLURAL NOUN _____

COLOR_____

SILLY WORD_____

ADJECTIVE_____

SAME TOWN _____

ADJECTIVE_____

MAD LIBS®
NEWSPAPER STORY

Last Thursday, two _____ men were
                              TOWN

_____ in a/an _____ field near
VERB ENDING IN "ING"   NOUN

_____ , Indiana. Suddenly, one of them said,
              TOWN

"Hey, _____ , look up there at that bright, silvery
              NAME OF PERSON (MALE)

_____ floating over our _____ !"
TYPE OF VEHICLE   PLURAL NOUN

And before his friend could reply, a powerful _____ light shot
                                                      COLOR

down and lifted them into a strange flying _____ . Inside,
                                                  NOUN

they were greeted by tiny green _____ and given a
                                  SOMETHING ALIVE (PLURAL)

dinner of French-fried _____ and _____ beans.
                          PLURAL NOUN   COLOR

Afterwards, they flew to the planet _____ and met the
                                          SILLY WORD

_____ inhabitants. Then the flying machine brought them
ADJECTIVE

back to _____ , Indiana. The men told our reporter
          SAME TOWN

that it was really a/an _____ experience.
                          ADJECTIVE

From MAD LIBS® FROM OUTER SPACE • Copyright © 1989 by Price Stern Sloan,
a division of Penguin Putnam Books for Young Readers, New York.

MAD LIBS® is fun to play with friends, but you can also play it by yourself! To begin with, DO NOT look at the story on the page below. Fill in the blanks on this page with the words called for. Then, using the words you have selected, fill in the blank spaces in the story.

Now you've created your own hilarious MAD LIBS® game!

STAR TRUCK

SILLY WORD_____

ADJECTIVE_____

NOUN _____

NAME OF PERSON (MALE)_____

PLURAL NOUN _____

ADJECTIVE_____

PERSON IN ROOM _____

ADVERB_____

PLURAL NOUN _____

NOUN _____

ADJECTIVE_____

ADJECTIVE_____

NOUN _____

NUMBER _____

SAME SILLY WORD _____

NOUN _____

MAD LIBS®
STAR TRUCK

Dear Mr. _____,
             SILLY WORD

My favorite TV show is that _____ adventure in
                        ADJECTIVE

outer space called "Star _____." You and Captain
                       NOUN

_____ are my favorite _____. When I watch
NAME OF PERSON (MALE)   PLURAL NOUN

this _____ show I sometimes feel I am actually on the
      ADJECTIVE

Star Ship _____ and I am going _____
        PERSON IN ROOM   ADVERB

into those far _____ of the Universe, where no
              PLURAL NOUN

_____ has ever gone before.
   NOUN

I like it when the _____ aliens try to trap you and your crew
            ADJECTIVE

and you use your _____ logical mind to outsmart them.
            ADJECTIVE

I go to all the "Star _____" conventions and buy all of the
            NOUN

little toys and dolls even though I am _____ years old. But the
            NUMBER

real reason I wrote to you, Mr. _____, is because
            SAME SILLY WORD

I want you to send me an autographed _____.
            NOUN

MAD LIBS® is fun to play with friends, but you can also play it by yourself! To begin with, DO NOT look at the story on the page below. Fill in the blanks on this page with the words called for. Then, using the words you have selected, fill in the blank spaces in the story.

Now you've created your own hilarious MAD LIBS® game!

ROCKETS

NOUN _____

NAME OF PERSON (MALE)_____

NOUN _____

PLURAL NOUN _____

ADJECTIVE_____

PLACE _____

TYPE OF LIQUID _____

VERB (PAST TENSE)_____

EXCLAMATION_____

PLURAL NOUN _____

ADJECTIVE_____

NOUN _____

CITY _____

NAME OF PERSON (FEMALE)_____

DEPARTMENT STORE_____

ADVERB_____

...covery of rocket power. Many years

a... _____ named _____
            NOUN   NAME OF PERSON (MALE)

bega... ...g with a long hollow _____ that had
                                        NOUN

an explos... mixture of sodium and _____ at one end.
                                          PLURAL NOUN

He put this _____ device on an inclined board and aimed
                  ADJECTIVE

it at _____. Then he poured hydrochloric _____ on
           PLACE   TYPE OF LIQUID

the sodium, and the whole thing _____ for ten minutes.
                                      VERB (PAST TENSE)

When he regained consciousness, he said, "_____!"
                                                    EXCLAMATION

and packed up his clothes and _____ and moved to
                                    PLURAL NOUN

Amsterdam, where he married a/an _____ widow who
                                        ADJECTIVE

owned a _____ shop.
              NOUN

Some years later, the world became aware of rockets when a scientist

at _____ University named _____ sent
         CITY   NAME OF PERSON (FEMALE)

off to _____ for one. And that is why today we are
         DEPARTMENT STORE

able to fly _____ to the moon.
                  ADVERB

From MAD LIBS® FROM OUTER SPACE • Copyright © 1989 by Price Stern Sloan,
a division of Penguin Putnam Books for Young Readers, New York.

MAD LIBS® is fun to play with friends, but you can also play it by yourself! To begin with, DO NOT look at the story on the page below. Fill in the blanks on this page with the words called for. Then, using the words you have selected, fill in the blank spaces in the story.

Now you've created your own hilarious MAD LIBS® game!

SOME OUTER SPACE POETRY

NOUN _____

NOUN _____

NOUN _____

ANIMAL _____

MUSICAL INSTRUMENT _____

NOUN _____

VERB (PAST TENSE)_____

NOUN _____

NOUN _____

NOUN _____

VERB (PAST TENSE)_____

MAD LIBS®
SOME OUTER SPACE POETRY

Twinkle, twinkle little _____,
                                 NOUN

How I wonder what you are.

Up above the _____ so high,
                  NOUN

Just like a/an _____ in the sky.
                 NOUN

Hey diddle diddle, the _____
                     ANIMAL

and the _____,
          MUSICAL INSTRUMENT

The cow jumped over the _____.
                    NOUN

The little dog _____ to see such sport,
            VERB (PAST TENSE)

And the _____ ran away with the spoon.
        NOUN

Star light, star bright, first _____ I see tonight.
                                NOUN

I wish I may, I wish I might,

Have the _____ I _____ tonight.
           NOUN   VERB (PAST TENSE)

From MAD LIBS® FROM OUTER SPACE • Copyright © 1989 by Price Stern Sloan,
a division of Penguin Putnam Books for Young Readers, New York.

MAD LIBS® is fun to play with friends, but you can also play it by yourself! To begin with, DO NOT look at the story on the page below. Fill in the blanks on this page with the words called for. Then, using the words you have selected, fill in the blank spaces in the story.

Now you've created your own hilarious MAD LIBS® game!

OUR UNIVERSE, SORT OF

ADJECTIVE _____

ADJECTIVE _____

FIRST NAME OF PERSON _____

NOUN _____

NUMBER _____

NOUN _____

PLURAL NOUN _____

ADVERB _____

NUMBER _____

ADJECTIVE _____

PLURAL NOUN _____

PLURAL NOUN _____

VERB ENDING IN "ING" _____

MAD LIBS®
OUR UNIVERSE, SORT OF

The Earth is a/an _____ little planet on the outer
ADJECTIVE

edge of a/an _____ galaxy called _____.
ADJECTIVE   FIRST NAME OF PERSON

The center of this galaxy is called the Milky _____, and it
NOUN

extends for _____ parsecs. A parsec is a metric _____
NUMBER   NOUN

that is used to measure the vast distances between _____.
PLURAL NOUN

There are a million billion planets in our galaxy, and they are all

_____ drawing away from each other at the rate of
ADVERB

_____ miles a year. The little _____ spots of light
NUMBER   ADJECTIVE

we see in the sky and which we call _____ are really
PLURAL NOUN

suns in distant solar systems. Each of these suns has dozens of huge

_____ spinning in orbit around it.
PLURAL NOUN

Now, that is the way it is, so you can stop _____ about
VERB ENDING IN "ING"

it. If you don't like the universe, you can always go someplace else.

From MAD LIBS® FROM OUTER SPACE • Copyright © 1989 by Price Stern Sloan,
a division of Penguin Putnam Books for Young Readers, New York.

MAD LIBS® is fun to play with friends, but you can also play it by yourself! To begin with, DO NOT look at the story on the page below. Fill in the blanks on this page with the words called for. Then, using the words you have selected, fill in the blank spaces in the story.

Now you've created your own hilarious MAD LIBS® game!

PAGES FROM A
MARTIAN GIFT CATALOG

ADJECTIVE _____

TYPE OF METAL _____

PLURAL NOUN_____

ADJECTIVE _____

TYPE OF APPLIANCE_____

TYPE OF LIQUID_____

NUMBER_____

PLURAL NOUN_____

NOUN _____

PLURAL NOUN_____

PLURAL NOUN_____

ADVERB _____

PART OF THE BODY _____

TYPE OF TOOL _____

SOMETHING STICKY _____

NOUN _____

ADJECTIVE _____

SOMETHING ALIVE (PLURAL)_____

MAD☺LIBS®
PAGES FROM A
MARTIAN GIFT CATALOG

Here is a really _____ bargain in solid _____

ADJECTIVE   TYPE OF METAL

_____ . These handsome but _____ gifts

PLURAL NOUN   ADJECTIVE

can be used to hold down your _____ while you're

TYPE OF APPLIANCE

having your morning cup of _____ . Guaranteed for

TYPE OF LIQUID

_____ eons and only fourteen gold _____ each.

NUMBER   PLURAL NOUN

Dress up your _____ room with one of these folding

NOUN

_____ . Comes with white enamel _____ and

PLURAL NOUN   PLURAL NOUN

is delivered _____ by Arcturian Express. Completely

ADVERB

assembled except for the _____ rest which is easily

PART OF THE BODY

installed with a/an _____ and some _____ .

TYPE OF TOOL   SOMETHING STICKY

A most welcome gift for the _____ Season that will

NOUN

bring hours of happiness to you and your _____ little

ADJECTIVE

_____ .

SOMETHING ALIVE (PLURAL)

From MAD LIBS® FROM OUTER SPACE • Copyright © 1989 by Price Stern Sloan,
a division of Penguin Putnam Books for Young Readers, New York.

MAD LIBS® is fun to play with friends, but you can also play it by yourself! To begin with, DO NOT look at the story on the page below. Fill in the blanks on this page with the words called for. Then, using the words you have selected, fill in the blank spaces in the story.

Now you've created your own hilarious MAD LIBS® game!

ALIENS ARE OUR FRIENDS

NOUN _____

ADJECTIVE _____

SOMETHING ROUND _____

ADJECTIVE _____

OCCUPATION _____

EXCLAMATION _____

PLURAL NOUN _____

ADJECTIVE _____

PLURAL NOUN _____

PLACE _____

TYPE OF FOOD (PLURAL) _____

ADJECTIVE _____

TYPE OF VEHICLE (PLURAL) _____

ADVERB _____

MAD LIBS®
ALIENS ARE OUR FRIENDS

If you run into an alien _____ who comes from some
                              NOUN

other _____ planet which revolves around a distant
         ADJECTIVE

_____ in another galaxy, do not be _____.
SOMETHING ROUND   ADJECTIVE

If it says, "Take me to your _____," you must act
                                OCCUPATION

friendly and say, " _____ !"
                      EXCLAMATION

Remember, extraterrestrial _____ are not necessarily
                              PLURAL NOUN

hostile. Many of them are _____ and all they want is to
                             ADJECTIVE

put you in one of their _____ and fly you off for a
                           PLURAL NOUN

vacation in _____. So offer them a few _____
              PLACE   TYPE OF FOOD (PLURAL)

or take them out to a movie. If you do, maybe they will tell you the

secret of _____ telepathy or how they power their
             ADJECTIVE

rocket _____. If you treat an extra-terrestrial
          TYPE OF VEHICLE (PLURAL)

_____ you may make a new friend.
     ADVERB

MAD LIBS® is fun to play with friends, but you can also play it by yourself! To begin with, DO NOT look at the story on the page below. Fill in the blanks on this page with the words called for. Then, using the words you have selected, fill in the blank spaces in the story.

Now you've created your own hilarious MAD LIBS® game!

IS SPACE TRAVEL POSSIBLE

VERB ENDING IN "ING" _____

NUMBER _____

NAME OF PERSON (FEMALE) _____

PIECE OF FURNITURE _____

VERB (PAST TENSE) _____

NOUN _____

NOUN _____

NOUN _____

PLURAL NOUN _____

ADJECTIVE _____

NUMBER _____

VERB ENDING IN "ING" _____

ADJECTIVE _____

PLURAL NOUN _____

PERSON IN ROOM _____

ANIMAL _____

ADJECTIVE _____

MAD⊙LIBS®
IS SPACE TRAVEL POSSIBLE

When people begin _____ in outer space, they
VERB ENDING IN "ING"

will have to spend _____ years just getting to the nearest solar
NUMBER

system, called _____. At first, travelers will
NAME OF PERSON (FEMALE)

probably be frozen and put in a/an _____. Then,
PIECE OF FURNITURE

when the ship arrives, the travelers will be _____.
VERB (PAST TENSE)

Eventually scientists may invent a/an _____ transporter
NOUN

like the one they used on the TV show, "_____ Trek."
NOUN

It will break down all parts of the human _____ into
NOUN

atoms and _____. Then these will be broadcast like
PLURAL NOUN

_____ TV waves and reassembled _____ miles
ADJECTIVE   NUMBER

away. If this doesn't work, engineers are _____
VERB ENDING IN "ING"

now, trying to perfect a/an _____ drive that will run a
ADJECTIVE

spaceship faster than the speed of _____. But of course
PLURAL NOUN

scientists such as _____ say this is a lot of
PERSON IN ROOM

_____ wash. So maybe humans should forget space travel
ANIMAL

and try to solve the _____ traffic problems on Earth.
ADJECTIVE

From MAD LIBS® FROM OUTER SPACE • Copyright © 1989 by Price Stern Sloan,
a division of Penguin Putnam Books for Young Readers, New York.

MAD LIBS® is fun to play with friends, but you can also play it by yourself! To begin with, DO NOT look at the story on the page below. Fill in the blanks on this page with the words called for. Then, using the words you have selected, fill in the blank spaces in the story.

Now you've created your own hilarious MAD LIBS® game!

LOOKING GOOD ON PLUTO

NUMBER _____

CITY _____

SOMETHING ALIVE _____

ADJECTIVE _____

ADJECTIVE _____

PLURAL NOUN _____

PLURAL NOUN _____

ADJECTIVE _____

TYPE OF LIQUID _____

ARTICLE OF CLOTHING _____

PLURAL NOUN _____

COLOR _____

PART OF THE FACE _____

PART OF THE FACE _____

PLURAL NOUN _____

MAD LIBS®
LOOKING GOOD ON PLUTO

On Pluto, the gravity is _____ times as strong as it is in
                              NUMBER

_____ . So if you are a young _____
         CITY   SOMETHING ALIVE

there and you want to look good, here is what you should do. First go

to a beauty parlor and get a/an _____ haircut by a/an
                                      ADJECTIVE

_____ Plutonian barber. Make sure he keeps your hair out
      ADJECTIVE

of your _____ so you can show off your _____ .
          PLURAL NOUN   PLURAL NOUN

This is the _____ fashion on Pluto today.
                  ADJECTIVE

Then spray yourself with _____ and put on an aluminum
                            TYPE OF LIQUID

foil _____ and high-heel _____ .
     ARTICLE OF CLOTHING   PLURAL NOUN

Makeup is as important on Pluto as it is on Earth, so put some bright

_____ lipstick on your _____ and use a nice
      COLOR   PART OF THE FACE

_____ shadow. If you follow this advice, you will get
   PART OF THE FACE

your picture on the covers of all their _____ .
                                            PLURAL NOUN

From MAD LIBS® FROM OUTER SPACE • Copyright © 1989 by Price Stern Sloan,
a division of Penguin Putnam Books for Young Readers, New York.

MAD LIBS® is fun to play with friends, but you can also play it by yourself! To begin with, DO NOT look at the story on the page below. Fill in the blanks on this page with the words called for. Then, using the words you have selected, fill in the blank spaces in the story.

Now you've created your own hilarious MAD LIBS® game!

LEGAL PROBLEMS ON VENUS

NOUN _____

NOUN _____

NOUN _____

PLURAL NOUN _____

PLURAL NOUN _____

ADJECTIVE _____

NOUN _____

NOUN _____

NOUN _____

EXCLAMATION _____

PART OF THE BODY _____

TYPE OF VEHICLE _____

MAD⊙LIBS®
LEGAL PROBLEMS
ON VENUS

QUESTION: What happens if I purchase a/an _____
NOUN

and then the government decides to build a/an

_____ right through my _____?
NOUN   NOUN

ANSWER: The value of all of your _____ will drop
PLURAL NOUN

and your _____ will probably stop
PLURAL NOUN

working due to the_____ noise. Frankly,
ADJECTIVE

you will be up the creek without a/an _____.
NOUN

QUESTION: I want to adopt a/an _____. How do
NOUN

I go about it?

ANSWER: You may adopt a/an _____ on Mars simply
NOUN

by looking at it and saying, " _____." But
EXCLAMATION

on Venus, you have to hop on one _____
PART OF THE BODY

at the same time, preferably while riding a/an

_____.
TYPE OF VEHICLE

MAD LIBS® is fun to play with friends, but you can also play it by yourself! To begin with, DO NOT look at the story on the page below. Fill in the blanks on this page with the words called for. Then, using the words you have selected, fill in the blank spaces in the story.

Now you've created your own hilarious MAD LIBS® game!

A LETTER WRITTEN BY A LONELY EXTRATERRESTRIAL

SILLY FIRST NAME _____

LAST NAME OF PERSON _____

ANOTHER LAST NAME_____

TYPE OF APPLIANCE _____

ADJECTIVE_____

PART OF THE BODY (PLURAL) _____

NOUN _____

NOUN _____

OCCUPATION _____

OCCUPATION _____

EXCLAMATION_____

PART OF THE BODY _____

ADJECTIVE_____

ADVERB_____

PLACE _____

PLURAL NOUN _____

VERB _____

MAD☉LIBS®
A LETTER WRITTEN BY A LONELY EXTRATERRESTRIAL

Dear _____ _____,
　　　　　SILLY FIRST NAME　　　LAST NAME OF PERSON

I am writing to you from the planet _____ because
　　　　　　　　　　　　　　　　　　　ANOTHER LAST NAME

I saw your picture on the electronic _____, and I
　　　　　　　　　　　　　　　　　　TYPE OF APPLIANCE

think you are very _____. You have the five prettiest
　　　　　　　　　ADJECTIVE

_____ I have ever seen. And your _____
PART OF THE BODY (PLURAL)　　　　　　　　　　　　　NOUN

is out of this galaxy. I certainly hope that you are a _____
　　　　　　　　　　　　　　　　　　　　　　　　　NOUN

of the opposite sex. If you are, and if you aren't a/an _____,
　　　　　　　　　　　　　　　　　　　　　　　OCCUPATION

then I would like you to be my _____. If you read this
　　　　　　　　　　　　　OCCUPATION

and your answer is "_____," then I will contact your
　　　　　　　　　EXCLAMATION

father, Darth Vader, and formally ask for your _____. My
　　　　　　　　　　　　　　　　　　　PART OF THE BODY

_____ father tells me that two can live as _____
ADJECTIVE　　　　　　　　　　　　　　　　　　　　ADVERB

as one, so we can afford to buy a little condo in _____
　　　　　　　　　　　　　　　　　　　　　PLACE

and settle down and raise some sweet little _____.
　　　　　　　　　　　　　　　　　　PLURAL NOUN

Please _____ to me right away and send a photograph.
　　　VERB

From MAD LIBS® FROM OUTER SPACE • Copyright © 1989 by Price Stern Sloan,
a division of Penguin Putnam Books for Young Readers, New York.

MAD LIBS® is fun to play with friends, but you can also play it by yourself! To begin with, DO NOT look at the story on the page below. Fill in the blanks on this page with the words called for. Then, using the words you have selected, fill in the blank spaces in the story.

Now you've created your own hilarious MAD LIBS® game!

A POLICE CALL ON MARS

PLURAL NOUN _____

SILLY NAME _____

NOUN _____

PLURAL NOUN _____

NUMBER _____

NAME OF PERSON (MALE) _____

ARTICLE OF CLOTHING _____

ADJECTIVE _____

PLURAL NOUN _____

VERB ENDING IN "ING" _____

VERB ENDING IN "ING" _____

NOUN _____

ADJECTIVE _____

NOUN _____

ADVERB _____

NOUN _____

SILLY WORD _____

ANOTHER SILLY WORD _____

MAD LIBS®
A POLICE CALL ON MARS

Calling all _____ . This is _____ ,
                    PLURAL NOUN   SILLY NAME

your Martian police _____ . All of you patrol
                              NOUN

_____ keep all _____ of your eyes peeled for a
      PLURAL NOUN   NUMBER

_____ . When last seen, he was wearing a double-
   NAME OF PERSON (MALE)

breasted _____ . He is wanted for questioning in a/an
              ARTICLE OF CLOTHING

_____ robbery and was seen by several _____
         ADJECTIVE   PLURAL NOUN

who state he was _____ and _____
                     VERB ENDING IN "ING"   VERB ENDING IN "ING"

in the vicinity of the state _____ house.
                                        NOUN

If you see this _____ _____ , approach
                        ADJECTIVE   NOUN

him _____ because he may be carrying a loaded
              ADVERB

_____ . Also, he has been known to use the alias
         NOUN

_____ the _____ . That is all.
      SILLY WORD   ANOTHER SILLY WORD

From MAD LIBS® FROM OUTER SPACE • Copyright © 1989 by Price Stern Sloan,
a division of Penguin Putnam Books for Young Readers, New York.